STRONG WOMAN, STRONG BUSINESS

How the Right Health Coach Can Help You
Feel Better, Live Stronger and ***Achieve Greater Success***

STRONG WOMAN, STRONG BUSINESS

How the Right Health Coach Can Help You
Feel Better, Live Stronger and ***Achieve Greater Success***

MUKUL NAGPAUL

Available on amazonkindle

Worldwide Published by

Pendown Press
PREMIUM BUSINESS PUBLISHER

PENDOWN PRESS LLP

An ISO 9001 & ISO 14001 Certified Co.,

Regd. Office: 3767A, Kanhaiya Nagar,

Tri Nagar, Delhi-110035

Ph.: 8130886000, 9650072927

E-mail: info@pendownpress.com

Branch Office: 1A/2A, 20, Hari Sadan, Ansari Road,

Daryaganj, New Delhi-110002

Ph.: 011-45794768

Website: PendownPress.com

Edition: 2025

Price: ₹ 299/-

ISBN: 978-81-989619-0-7

Layout and Cover Designed by Pendown Graphics Team

Dedication

This book is dedicated to:

My parents: For their unwavering support in every aspect of my life. They have instilled in me the values of humility and service to others, which continue to guide me every day.

My wife, Himani: My strength, my backbone, and the one who completes me. Her unconditional support has been the cornerstone of everything I do. She gives me the courage to dream bigger and the confidence to make a meaningful impact in the world.

My Guru, Akshar Yadav: I am truly blessed to have found a Guru who illuminated the blind spots in my life, guided me through them, and showed me the path I had long been searching for. His wisdom and presence have brought clarity and purpose to my journey.

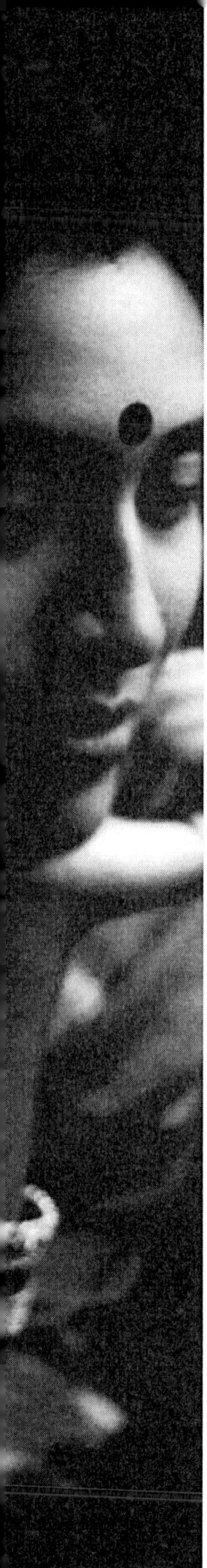

Table of Contents

Acknowledgements i

Foreword iii

Preface vii

My Journey Of Purpose xi
Who Am I & Why You Can Trust Me

Let's Get The Basics Right xv

Chapter 1:
Why Waking Up Early Isn't for Everyone 1

Chapter 2:
Meditation Isn't Always the Answer to Stress 5

Chapter 3:
Carbs at Night Don't Always Make You Fat 9

Chapter 4:
Morning Workouts Aren't Magic 13

Chapter 5:
You Don't Have to Skip Dining Out to Get Fit 17

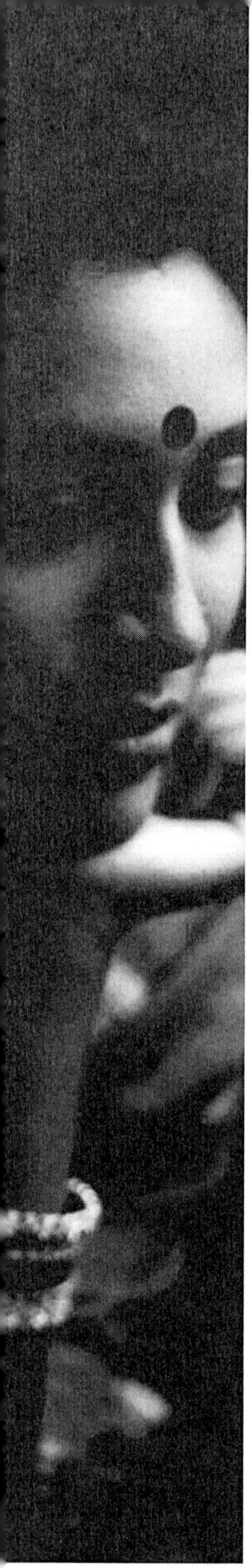

Chapter 6:

Intermittent Fasting Isn't for Everyone 21

Chapter 7:

More Protein Doesn't Always Mean More Muscle 25

A Quick Recap for Ready-Reference & Some Choices 29

Ackowledgements

I would like to express my sincere gratitude to the individuals who have significantly shaped my journey in fitness and education:

Fabio Comana, thank you for making complex subjects like biology and the body's energy systems so accessible and easy to understand. Your intelligent, well-informed, and practical approach greatly enhanced my ability to absorb and apply knowledge effectively.

Suzanne Hosley, my horizons in the fitness industry expanded immensely thanks to the Asia Fitness Conference you organized. Your dedication to elevating fitness education in the region has had a lasting impact on me.

Lawrence Biscontini, you brought joy and fun into the process of learning fitness. More importantly, you taught me the importance of using our knowledge with empathy and care for those we train.

Jonathan Ross, through your teachings, I discovered how to make fitness fun. You helped me realize that when exercise is enjoyable, people are more likely to embrace and stick with it.

Dr. Cam McDonald, you taught me the science of personalisation and how important it is to move from general recommendations to customised ones.

Sumaya Dalmia, you showed me how to challenge industry norms and prioritize real results for trainees over sales numbers. You taught me the true value of applying technical knowledge to create meaningful impact, instead of merely focusing on hitting PT sales targets.

❐ ❐ ❐

Foreword

The world of health is undergoing a profound transformation. For decades, we've been conditioned to accept a one-size-fits-all approach to health and wellness, generic advice, broad-spectrum solutions, and fleeting trends that often fail to address the unique needs of the individual. But that era is coming to an end. The future of health lies in precision health and medicine, a paradigm that recognizes and celebrates the individuality of every human being. And the faster we embrace this shift, the better off we'll all be.

Yet, as with any revolution, there are challenges. One of the greatest obstacles to this new paradigm is the resistance of health professionals who cling to outdated beliefs about what constitutes "best health." They rely on generalized methods, hesitant to let go of practices that no longer serve the diverse needs of their clients. But amidst this resistance, there are pioneers, visionaries who are not only ready for change but are actively leading the charge. These are the health professionals who are here to serve, not themselves, but the individuals in their care.

Mukul is one of these extraordinary leaders. A precision health coach with a deep commitment to empowering others, Mukul embodies the very essence of this new paradigm. In this world of precision health, individuals are no longer reduced to statistics or averages. Instead, they are seen, heard, and supported as the unique beings they are. Every nuance of their biological, emotional, and environmental makeup is accounted for, creating a truly personalized approach to health and well-being.

This is made possible through cutting-edge medical AI and precision health technology, but technology alone is not enough. It takes a health professional with the heart, knowledge, and dedication to guide individuals through this transformative process. Mukul is exactly that kind of professional. Having worked closely with Mukul over the years, I can confidently say that his unwavering focus on the health and outcomes of his clients is unparalleled. His ego never interferes with his mission, and his passion for helping others achieve their best lives is both inspiring and contagious.

This book is more than just a guide: it's a gateway.

Within these pages, you'll find not only the science and principles of precision health but also real-world case studies that demonstrate its life-changing potential. You'll see how individuals, once lost in the maze of generic advice and trial-and-error solutions, have found clarity, vitality, and empowerment through this approach. These stories are a testament to what's possible when the right tools are placed in the hands of the right professionals.

For female entrepreneurs, this book is particularly powerful. As leaders, creators, and innovators, you often carry the weight of the world on your shoulders. Your health and well-being are not just personal priorities—they are the foundation of your success and impact. Precision health offers you the opportunity to optimize your energy, focus, and resilience, allowing you to show up as your best self in every area of your life.

But the insights in this book are not limited to entrepreneurs. They are universal. Whether you're a parent, a professional, or simply someone seeking to live your healthiest, happiest life, the principles and practices outlined here are for you. They are for anyone ready to step into a new era of health, one where you are no longer at the mercy of guesswork or fleeting trends but are empowered with the knowledge and tools to thrive.

Gone are the days when achieving optimal health required endless specialists, exorbitant costs, and years of frustration. With the guidance of a skilled, open-minded, and compassionate health professional like Mukul, armed with the most advanced precision health technology, you can achieve results that were once thought impossible.

This book is your starting point. It's an invitation to understand yourself on a deeper level, to embrace the power of personalized health, and to take the first step toward a life of vitality and fulfillment. Mukul's insights, stories, and expertise will not only educate you but also inspire you to take action.

This is the new paradigm of health. And Mukul is one of its leading lights. Let this book be your guide, your motivation, and your inspiration to unlock the potential within you. The journey begins here.

Dr Cam McDonald PhD

CEO Precision Health Alliance

APD; AEP; FASLM

Preface

The Why, How & What Of This Book

Are you a female entrepreneur who feels like Maa Durga, managing life with eight hands: juggling business, family, health, and a thousand other responsibilities, all at once?

You're constantly in motion, giving your best to your work, your loved ones, and everyone who depends on you. Yet, in the rush to keep every ball in the air, your own well-being often slips through your fingers.

If you're feeling stretched thin, exhausted, or disconnected from yourself, you're not alone. So many women like you are living life in overdrive, trying to be everything to everyone, but rarely pausing to care for themselves.

This book is intended as your gentle reminder and your practical guide to put yourself back at the center of your own story.

Inside, you'll find:

- Real strategies
- Inspiring stories
- And a supportive roadmap

To help you nurture your health, boost your energy, and find joy in both your business and your home.

Yes, you have the strength of a goddess, but you don't have to do it all alone.

Let this book be your companion as you reclaim balance, fulfillment, and the vibrant life you truly deserve.

This book was born out of a personal loss and a determination to prevent that loss for others. Recently, I was about to start working on my best friend's mother's health. We were just getting ready to begin, but before we could, we lost her to cancer. It hit me deeply, and for a long time, I felt like I had failed her.

But that pain sparked something inside me, a fire to help more people take control of their health before it's too late. I knew I had to act fast and find the most powerful way to reach and inspire crores of people to live healthier lives.

After researching all the available media, I realized that a book is the most powerful tool; it's like my messenger, reaching readers in far-off places even without me.

This book is my way of empowering you to find answers to all the questions you face about your health.

Even after helping thousands of people on their health journeys, I still felt a deep sense of unfulfillment. While 80% of my trainees achieved exceptional results, the remaining 20% struggled to see the desired outcomes, even when using the best science available in the health and fitness industry.

This led me to dig deeper, research the missing link, and uncover the truth: the missing piece is working with your natural biology, environment, and hormones. Traditional approaches often ignore this, but by addressing it, you can achieve long-lasting results in a healthy way and with less effort.

If you're serious about transforming your health, you can't afford to ignore this book. It's time to move beyond the surface and discover the science that will truly change your life.

In this book, you will learn:

1. The best time for you to wake up
2. The best method for you to reduce stress
3. The best way to eat
4. The best time to exercise
5. How to enjoy life while being productive

❒ ❒ ❒

My Journey Of Purpose

Who Am I & Why You Can Trust Me

Hi, I'm Mukul Nagpaul, and I was born and brought up in Ludhiana.

Since childhood, I've been both athletic and studious. I played Badminton at the All-India level.

When it was time to choose my future, I realized that working in my father's business didn't bring me joy. Instead, I found my happiness in helping others achieve their health and fitness goals.

That's when I discovered my life's purpose: that I am a Karam Yogi, born to help people become healthy and fit. At 18 years of age, this realization led me to join a gym, and while exercising, my wrist began to hurt, so I told my coach that my wrist hurt, and he just said "No Pain Gain", so I continued exercising, and my wrist got dislocated. That day, I decided that I would become a highly educated Fitness Coach and wouldn't let injuries like this happen to anyone.

This commitment brought me to Delhi to study health and fitness, leading to gaining knowledge from top institutes and getting certifications like:

1. Certified Health Coach from Precision Health Alliance, Australia
2. Certified Personal Trainer from the American Council on Exercise

3. Certified Online Trainer from the Online Training Academy
4. CPR and First Aid from the Indian Red Cross Society
5. CPR from the American Heart Association

In 2013, I met my soulmate, Himani, who helped me convert my goal into a mission to empower over 1 crore people to live a healthy lifestyle, and we experimented on ourselves, going from being overweight to getting six-pack abs in just 28 days.

However, we realised that while we were the fittest in our lives at that time, but were not happy as we avoided going to family functions and meeting friends. And even if we went out, then we carried our own food, which impacted our relationship with food, and when we started leading a normal life, we gained all the weight back.,

This impacted our self-confidence, and that's why we realised the importance of mental training, which led me to participate in Endurance events where I finished events like

- 42.2 km in the Ladakh Marathon, which is the highest marathon in the World
- 42.2 Kms in the Mumbai Marathon
- The Ironman Triathlon in Malaysia, which is the toughest one-day endurance race in the World, where you have to do 3.8 km Swimming, 180 km Cycling, and 42.2 km running within 17 hours.

Then we used the same mental fitness for our trainees and were able to transform thousands, leading to getting awarded as

- No.1 Personal Trainer in Asia at the Asia Fitness Conference
- Online Training Expert by the Fitness Excellence Awards

- Excellent Athlete by the World Fitness Culture

And our articles got featured in top magazines and newspapers like Vogue, Times of India, Hindustan Times, The Hindu, Grazia, etc

For the past 17 years, I've worked with thousands of people, helping them build high-performing minds and bodies. My trainees trust me because I leave no stone unturned in helping them achieve their goals—whether it's looking great to boost their confidence for closing more high-ticket deals, reducing stress, or simply staying fit to enjoy the life they've worked so hard to build. Does that sound like something you'd be interested in?

I think that's a yes, I heard. Well then, let's get started.

Stay excited and stay with me....

❑ ❑ ❑

Let's Get The Basics Right

Let me share some good and bad news with you.

- **The bad news is that all the gurus claiming their method is the best way to get healthy are wrong—**

There's no one-size-fits-all solution. At best, a particular method will work for 40-50% of people. If you're among the lucky ones it works for, that's great! But what if you're part of the 50-60% of non-responders?

- **The good news is that there's a way to understand what will work specifically for you.**

Let me introduce you to the *Six HealthType™*, as you'll likely fall into one of these categories, and before we can even begin working on your health, it's important for you to know what your body and mind want and respond to. Then we'll take things forward from there.

1. **Activators:** *Dominated by adrenaline* and testosterone, Activators are like cats, energetic, action-oriented, and "do first, think later" individuals who thrive on movement and variety. For them, exercise and food are the most critical factors for health. Interestingly, most health and fitness advice in the industry is geared toward Activators, which is why you often hear, "Just work on your food and start exercising." But as you'll soon discover, this approach doesn't work for everyone.
2. **Connectors:** *With oxytocin,* the "love hormone," as their dominant hormone, Connectors are like puppies, bursting

with energy when they're with loved ones but needing time to recharge afterward. Social and expressive, they value relationships and emotional connections. For Connectors, feeling connected to a tribe or community is essential for long-term success. Their health thrives when they focus on their mental well-being and nurturing their relationships.

3. **Guardians:** *Dominated by prolactin,* the "care hormone," Guardians are like bears, saving energy during the summer to care for their family in the winter. Dependable and family-oriented, they prioritize stability and routine, often putting their loved ones first and their own needs last. For Guardians, good nutrition and ensuring their loved ones are safe and healthy are the most important aspects of their health journey.
4. **Diplomats:** *With serotonin,* the "pleasure hormone," as their dominant hormone, Diplomats are like buffaloes, enjoying life at their own pace. Rushing toward goals or deadlines stresses them out, leading to unhappiness. Calm and analytical, they excel in stable environments and value close relationships. For Diplomats, creating a comfortable and stress-free environment at work and home, while tapping into their inner genius, is key to their health and happiness.
5. **Sensors:** *Dominated by vasopressin,* the opposite of the love hormone oxytocin, Sensors are like birds—independent and protective of their personal space. They don't trust easily and thrive on creativity and intellectual pursuits. For Sensors, having a home and workspace that suits their needs and working on their mental clarity are vital for reducing stress and improving health.

6. **Crusaders:** *With dopamine,* the "instant satisfaction hormone," as their dominant hormone, Crusaders are like horses with blinkers—laser-focused on their goals. While this drive makes them disciplined and goal-oriented leaders, it can sometimes create challenges in achieving work-life balance. For Crusaders, connecting their health goals to their life's main objectives and using their inner genius to stay efficient is the top priority.

This book and your understanding of the various Health Types will transform the way you think about health.

It's not just another guide full of generic tips that work for a few and fail the rest. Instead, it exposes the truth behind 7 common health beliefs that often mislead more than they help.

These widespread recommendations, like waking up early, cutting carbs at night, or doing meditation for stress, are well-meaning but dangerously oversimplified.

The truth is: health is not one-size-fits-all.

Through science-backed insights and powerful personal stories, you'll discover how to align your lifestyle with your unique biology. Once you understand your own body, you'll realize how easy, enjoyable, and sustainable good health can truly be.

❒ ❒ ❒

Chapter 1

WHY WAKING UP EARLY ISN'T FOR EVERYONE

FIND YOUR NATURAL RHYTHM AND STOP FEELING "LAZY"

I hate to tell you this, but most motivational books and videos are lying when they say you can't be successful unless you wake up before the rest of the world.

The idea that "early to bed and early to rise" is the ultimate path to success is a myth that simply doesn't work for everyone. The Key is to finding and following your own body rhythm.

Dr. Shilpa's Journey From "Lazy" to Thriving

[How honoring her body clock transformed her confidence]

Take the case of Dr. Shilpa, a dedicated Diplomat HealthType^{TM}.

Since childhood, she was forced to wake up at 5 a.m., even though her body and mind never truly felt awake until much later in the morning.

Family and teachers labeled her as lazy, and over time, she began to believe it herself. The constant struggle to fit into someone else's routine chipped away at her self-confidence, making her feel inadequate and out of place.

When Dr. Shilpa finally learned to honor her natural rhythm, everything changed.

We worked together to adjust her sleep and wake times, allowing her to rise when her body was ready.

Almost immediately, her energy soared, her self-esteem blossomed, and she began to embrace her unique biology.

With this newfound confidence, she achieved greater success in her career and felt more connected to her family and herself.

If you've ever felt the sting of being misunderstood or the pressure to fit into a mold that just doesn't suit you, you're not alone. So many women, especially those building businesses and families, carry the weight of these expectations. You're told that discipline means sacrificing your own needs, that success is only for those who follow the "right" routine. But what if your right routine looks different? What if your power lies in honoring your own rhythm, not someone else's?

The truth is, for HealthTypes™ like Connectors, Guardians, and Diplomats, who are naturally more inclined to be night

owls, forcing an early bedtime and wake-up routine can disrupt their biological rhythms, leaving them groggy, unproductive, and out of sync. These types often perform better when they honor their later energy peaks and allow themselves to wind down naturally.

On the other hand, HealthTypes™ like Sensors, Crusaders, and Activators are biologically wired to be early risers, thriving on the structure and energy that comes with starting their day early. For them, an early-to-bed, early-to-rise routine aligns perfectly with their natural rhythms, helping them feel energized, focused, and productive.

Success isn't about following a universal rule; it's about understanding your HealthTypes™ and aligning your sleep-wake cycle with your body's natural design.

When you embrace who you truly are, you unlock the energy, confidence, and clarity you need to thrive on your own terms. Remember, your journey is yours alone, and the world needs the version of you that feels most alive.

❒ ❒ ❒

Chapter 2

MEDITATION ISN'T ALWAYS THE ANSWER TO STRESS

MANAGE STRESS ACCORDING TO YOUR HEALTHTYPE™

You've probably heard it a thousand times: "Just meditate and breathe, stress will melt away."

But what if I told you that meditation, while powerful for many, isn't the magic solution for everyone?

Moving Instead of Meditating

[Why stillness increased Nisha's stress, and movement set her free]

Take Nisha, for example, **a dynamic Crusader HealthType™** and a successful hotelier. Her days were a whirlwind of managing staff, handling guests, and putting out fires at every turn. When she attended a wellness retreat, **she was encouraged to meditate to reduce her stress.**

However, **every time she tried, her mind raced even more, and her stress levels actually increased.** Friends insisted she **must be "doing meditation wrong," because how could meditation possibly make things worse?**

But Nisha wasn't doing anything wrong; **she was simply following advice that didn't fit her unique biology.**

When we worked together, **we swapped out meditation for movement.** Instead of sitting still, **Nisha went for brisk walks or quick runs whenever she felt overwhelmed.**

- The results were immediate:
- Her mind cleared,
- Her stress melted away,

And she became noticeably calmer, even in the most challenging situations at work.

By honoring her natural need for movement, Nisha transformed her stress into strength and excelled in her demanding role.

If you've **ever felt frustrated or even guilty because the "right" stress relief technique didn't work for you, you're not alone.** So many women, especially those juggling businesses and families, feel like they're failing when the advice that's supposed to help only makes things harder. It's easy to question yourself, to wonder if you're broken or missing some secret ingredient everyone else seems to have. But **the truth is, you're not broken, you're unique.** Your body and mind are wired in a way that deserves respect, not shame.

Meditation is a wonderful tool for feeling connected to yourself, but if you're using it to beat stress, you might be surprised, it doesn't work for everyone.

- For HealthType™ like **Crusaders**, meditation can actually heighten anxiety when stress is high, making **movement a far better way** to release tension.
- **Activators**, who often feel stress as joint pain in the lower back or knees, benefit most from **high-intensity activities** like climbing stairs or punching a bag.
- **Connector** need to lean into their social nature; **spending time with loved ones or playing with a pet** can work wonders.
- **Guardians**, who tend to put family first, find relief by carving out **some much-needed "me time."**
- **Diplomats**, with their calm and steady nature, **can benefit from a spa day** to release serotonin and relax.
- **Sensors**, who thrive on focus and detail, can find peace by **retreating to a quiet corner with a favorite book**.

The truth is, stress management isn't one-size-fits-all.

Your HealthType™ determines the best way to unwind and restore balance.

When you honor your unique needs, you'll discover the most effective path to calm, clarity, and resilience. And in that space, you'll find the strength to lead, create, and care for others without losing yourself along the way.

❒ ❒ ❒

Chapter 3

Carbs at Night Don't Always Make You Fat

The Truth About When and What Your Body Needs

You've probably heard it before: "Cut carbs at night if you want to lose weight." It's a popular piece of advice, but the **truth is, it doesn't work for everyone.**

Sleep, Not Starvation, Burned Fat

(Adding carbs at night helped her lose weight and sleep better)

Take Madhuri, for example, an energetic **Activator HealthType™** and a successful bag manufacturer. Eager to shed a few kilos, **she followed her nutritionist's advice to reduce carbs at dinner**. But **instead of feeling lighter, she found herself tossing and turning at night, unable**

to get restful sleep. The lack of sleep left her stressed and frustrated, and **to her surprise, she actually gained weight instead of losing it.**

When we looked at her routine, it was clear that her body needed more fuel in the evening. We added moderate carbs back into her dinner.

Almost immediately, her sleep improved. She woke up feeling refreshed, her stress levels dropped, and she lost 2 kilos in just one week, simply by listening to her body's needs.

If you've ever stared at the ceiling at 2 a.m., wondering why your best efforts aren't working, you know how lonely and discouraging that can feel. As women entrepreneurs, you are used to pushing through, following the rules, and sacrificing comfort for results. But sometimes, the rules just don't fit. Sometimes, what your body needs is different from what the world tells you. And that's not a failure—it's a sign of your individuality and strength.

The idea that reducing carbs at night is the key to weight loss is a common myth.

- **For HealthType™ like Activators and Sensors,** who have **fast metabolisms** and burn through energy quickly, **cutting carbs at night can leave them feeling fatigued, restless,** or even trigger late-night cravings that derail their progress.
- **Crusaders**, with their disciplined and goal-driven nature, **also need steady energy** to fuel their routines, **making strict carb restriction at night less effective.**

- **On the other hand, reducing carbs at night works well for HealthTypes™ like Guardians and Diplomats**, who have slower metabolisms and a natural tendency to conserve energy. For them, this approach helps prevent fat storage and supports weight loss.
- **Connectors can also benefit**, as long as it doesn't interfere with their enjoyment of meals or social connections.

There's no one-size-fits-all solution.

Your HealthType™ determines how your body processes food, and understanding this is the real key to sustainable weight loss.

When you honor your unique biology, you'll find a path that works for you—and finally see the results you've been working for. And in that moment, you'll realize that true success comes from trusting yourself, not just following the crowd.

❒ ❒ ❒

Chapter 4

Morning Workouts Aren't Magic

Discover the Time Your Body Actually Loves to Move

You've probably heard that early morning is the best time to exercise. But the **truth is, this advice doesn't work for everyone.**

Evening Workouts Changed the Game

(Shifting her routine unleashed energy and rapid fat loss)

Take Maninder, for example, a **creative Diplomat HealthType™** and a talented fashion designer. Determined to get fit, **she signed up for high-intensity boot camps at dawn**, pushing herself through grueling workouts before sunrise.

Instead of feeling energized, Maninder **found herself completely drained after each session, with no energy left for the rest of her busy day. To make things worse, she started gaining weight instead of losing it.**

Her **trainer accused her of cheating on her diet,** but Maninder knew she was following her plan to the letter.

When we looked closer, it was clear that her body simply wasn't built for high-intensity exercise first thing in the morning.

We switched her workouts to the evening, allowing her body to wake up naturally and build energy throughout the day.

The results were dramatic:

Maninder **lost 5 kilos in just three weeks,** and her **energy and productivity soared.** She finally felt strong, focused, and in sync with her own rhythm.

If you've ever been misunderstood or doubted yourself because you didn't fit the "ideal" fitness mold, you're not alone.

As women entrepreneurs, you're often told to push harder, wake up earlier, and hustle more, no matter how you feel inside.

But what if your body's wisdom is quietly asking for something different?

What if honoring your own rhythm is the missing piece to unlocking your true strength?

Early morning workouts are often touted as the best time to exercise, but this simply doesn't hold true for all HealthType™.

- **For HealthType™ like Connectors, Guardians, and Diplomats,** whose bodies are **naturally slower to wake up** and prefer a steady, calm start to the day, early morning exercise can feel exhausting and counterproductive, leaving them drained rather than energized.
- **Even Sensors**, with their analytical and detail-oriented nature, **may not align with early morning workouts,** as their mental and physical energy often peaks later in the day, making evening or mid-morning sessions more effective.
- On the other hand, for HealthTypes™ like **Activators and Crusaders, early morning workouts can be a game-changer.** Activators, with their high-energy, action-oriented nature, thrive on the adrenaline and focus that comes with starting their day with movement.
- **Crusaders**, who are disciplined and goal-driven, **often find that morning exercise aligns perfectly with their structured routines**, helping them stay on track and feel accomplished before the day begins.

The truth is, there's no universal "best" time to work out. Your HealthType™ determines when your body is primed for peak performance, ensuring exercise feels energizing, not depleting.

When you listen to your body and trust your own timing, you'll discover a new level of power, confidence, and joy in movement, one that fits your life, your business, and your dreams.

❒ ❒ ❒

This material is for individual coaching inspiration only and does not teach or certify any methodology. For training or teaching others, a separate license is required.

Chapter 5

YOU DON'T HAVE TO SKIP DINING OUT TO GET FIT

STAY SOCIAL AND STILL ACHIEVE YOUR HEALTH GOALS

You've probably been told that if you want to get healthy, you need to stop eating out with friends and family. But **this advice just doesn't work for everyone.**

Losing Weight Without Missing Life

(How dining out helped her stay connected and consistent)

Take Anjali, for example, a **Connector HealthType™** and a talented makeup advisor. Anjali **loved going out with friends, sharing meals,** and building relationships over good food.

When **she was told to stop eating out and stick to only home-cooked meals to lose weight,** she gave it her best shot.

But instead of feeling healthier, **she felt anxious and isolated.** Her **happiness dipped,** and despite her efforts, **the weight wouldn't budge.**

When we looked at what really mattered to her, it was clear that social connection was non-negotiable.

We encouraged Anjali to keep going out with friends, but taught her how to balance her food choices while dining out.

She learned how to enjoy her favorite outings without guilt, making mindful decisions that fit her goals.

The results were incredible: **in just four weeks, Anjali lost 7 kilos, felt genuinely happier,** and her increased networking even led to more profits in her business.

If you've ever felt torn between your health goals and your need for connection, you know how heavy that choice can feel. As women entrepreneurs, your networks and relationships are often the heartbeat of your businesses and your lives.

Being told to give up those joyful moments can feel like being asked to choose between your dreams and your happiness.

The truth is, you shouldn't have to sacrifice one for the other.

The idea that you have to stop eating out with friends and family to achieve your health goals is a myth that doesn't work for everyone.

- **For HealthTypes™ like Connectors,** who thrive on emotional and social connection, cutting out meals with loved ones can feel isolating and counterproductive, as their well-being is deeply tied to shared experiences.
- **Activators,** who are action-oriented and spontaneous, may also find the rigidity of avoiding social dining stifling, making it harder to stay consistent with their goals. **Sensors,** who are detail-oriented and prefer control, may not need to stop eating out entirely but instead benefit from planning ahead or choosing environments where they can make mindful decisions.
- **On the other hand, HealthTypes™ like Guardians and Diplomats**, who value routine and stability, may benefit from reducing social dining, as it allows them to maintain control over their food choices and avoid the temptations that often come with eating out.
- **Crusaders,** with their disciplined and goal-driven nature, may also align with this approach, as it supports their structured routines and focus on results.

The truth is, your HealthType™ determines how you can best balance your social life and health goals.

Success comes from tailoring your approach, not following blanket rules. When you honor both your need for connection and your commitment to health, you create a life that's not only sustainable but deeply fulfilling, one where you can celebrate your wins with the people who matter most.

❐ ❐ ❐

Chapter 6

Intermittent Fasting Isn't for Everyone

Why Some Bodies Need Nourishment, Not Restriction

You've probably heard that intermittent fasting is the ultimate way to lose weight and get healthy. **But the truth is, it's not the best fit for everyone.**

Ditching Fasting, Healing Her Gut

[Steady meals and stress relief finally melted her belly fat]

Take Supriya, for example, **a Sensor HealthType™** and a talented interior designer. Supriya was naturally slim but **struggled with stubborn belly fat.**

Hoping to target it, she started intermittent fasting, skipping meals and eating in a tight window.

Instead of seeing results, her gut health took a nosedive.

She couldn't digest food properly, felt bloated, and her energy crashed. Her gut, which acts as the body's second brain, was missing out on the good bacteria it needed, and the fasting routine only made things worse.

When we took a closer look, **it was clear that Supriya's body needed steady nourishment. We switched her to three balanced meals and two snacks a day,** and also worked on managing her stress, which was a big contributor to her belly fat. With this new approach, her digestion improved, **her energy returned, and her belly fat finally melted away.**

If you've ever felt frustrated by a diet that everyone else seems to swear by, you're not alone. As women entrepreneurs, you're used to experimenting, adapting, and doing whatever it takes to reach your goals. But sometimes, following the crowd can leave you feeling more lost than empowered. It's easy to blame yourself when a "miracle" solution doesn't work, but the truth is, your body's needs are unique—and that's something to honor, not fight against.

The idea that intermittent fasting is the best diet for everyone is a myth that doesn't hold true for all HealthTypes™.

- **For HealthType™ like Activators, Crusaders, and Sensors,** who have fast metabolisms and need consistent energy to fuel their high-performance lifestyles, skipping meals can leave them feeling fatigued, irritable, and unfocused.
- **Connectors,** who thrive on emotional and social connection,

may also struggle with intermittent fasting, as rigid eating windows can disrupt their enjoyment of shared meals and social experiences.

- On the other hand, intermittent fasting can work well for **HealthType™ like Guardians and Diplomats,** who have slower metabolisms and benefit from longer breaks between meals to optimize digestion and prevent fat storage.

The truth is, no single diet works for everyone. Your HealthType™ determines how your body responds to fasting, and understanding this is **the key to finding a sustainable and effective approach.**

When you listen to your body and trust its signals, you'll discover a path to health that feels natural, empowering, and truly your own.

❒ ❒ ❒

Chapter 7

More Protein Doesn't Always Mean More Muscle

How to Eat for Strength Without the Bloating or Burnout

You've probably been told that a high-protein diet is the only way to build muscle and recover from workouts. **But this advice doesn't work for everyone.**

When Less Protein Meant Better Recovery

[How adjusting her macros brought lightness, energy, and results]

Take Surbhi, for example, **a Guardian HealthType™** and a dedicated architect. She worked out hard and **followed the**

common advice to load up on protein to speed up her recovery.

Instead of feeling stronger, she started gaining weight, felt constantly bloated, and her digestion became uncomfortable.

The high-protein diet left her feeling sluggish and inflamed, making it harder to bounce back after exercise.

When we took a closer look at her routine, it was clear that her body needed a different approach. We reduced her protein intake to a manageable level and balanced it with healthy carbs and fats.

- The change was almost immediate:
- Her inflammation went away
- Her digestion improved,

And her recovery from workouts actually got faster.

Surbhi felt lighter, more energetic, and finally started seeing the results she wanted.

If you've ever felt frustrated by doing everything "right" and still not seeing results, you're not alone. As women entrepreneurs, you're used to pushing through discomfort, trusting the experts, and hoping that hard work will pay off. But sometimes, the advice that works for others can leave you feeling worse, not better. It's easy to question your own efforts, to wonder if you're missing something essential, when in reality, your body is simply asking for a different approach.

The idea that you need a high-protein diet to achieve your health and fitness goals is a myth that doesn't work for all HealthTypes™.

- **For HealthTypes™ like Guardians and Diplomats,** too much protein can lead to inflammation and stress on the body. Their systems do better with moderate protein, balanced with carbs and fats to support recovery and overall health.
- **On the other hand, HealthTypes™ like Activators, Crusaders, Sensors, and Connectors** can thrive on higher protein intake, as their bodies are well-equipped to process it and use it effectively for muscle recovery and performance.

The truth is, your HealthType™ determines how much protein your body truly needs.

Understanding this is the key to optimizing your health and performance—without compromising your well-being. When you listen to your body and honor its unique needs, you'll find strength, resilience, and results that feel right for you—not just for everyone else.

❒ ❒ ❒

A Quick Recap for Ready-Reference & Some Choices

This book is your ultimate guide to understanding that health is not a one-size-fits-all journey. It's time to move beyond generic advice and discover what truly works for you.

Here's what we have covered in the book. You can use this section as a ready reference and then quickly go to the chapter you want to revisit:

- **The Best Time for You to Wake Up:** Understand how your unique HealthType™ determines whether you're an early riser or a night owl, and how aligning with your natural rhythm can boost your productivity and energy.
- **The Best Method to Reduce Stress:** Personalized stress-management techniques tailored to your HealthType™, whether it's meditation, movement, social connection, or quiet time.
- **The Best Way to Eat:** Discover how your body processes food based on your biology and hormones, and why certain diets work for some but not for others.
- **The Best Time to Exercise:** Find out when your body is primed for peak performance, ensuring your workouts are energizing and effective.
- **How to Enjoy Life While Being Productive:** Learning how to balance your health goals with your lifestyle, responsibilities, and relationships, so you can thrive without sacrificing joy.

With this book, we delved deep into the six HealthType™: Activators, Connectors, Guardians, Diplomats, Sensors, and Crusaders, helping you uncover the unique blueprint for your health.

By understanding your biology, hormones, and natural tendencies, you finally have the ability to achieve long-lasting results in a way that feels effortless and aligned with who you are.

But more than that, **this book is an invitation to trust yourself again**. As a woman entrepreneur, you juggle countless roles and expectations, often putting your own needs last.

This book offers permission as well as guidance to listen to your body, honor your instincts, and create a life where health and happiness go hand in hand.

You deserve a path that celebrates your individuality, supports your dreams, and empowers you to show up as your best self, at work, at home, and everywhere in between.

Are you ready to transform your health and life?

Your journey starts now.

Now you have two choices:

1. You can use the information in this book to start your own journey: apply what you've learned, experiment, and work towards your health goals step by step.

OR

2. If you want speedy and smooth results alongside personal guidance, reach out for a 1-on-1 call with me.

In this 45-minute session:

I'll help you understand your body and hormones better, so losing weight, boosting your energy, and balancing work, family, and health becomes a piece of cake.

Normally, this session is priced at INR 25,000, but as a thank you for being a reader, it's my gift to you.

Ready to make your transformation easier and more enjoyable?

Scan the QR Code below to claim your complimentary session.

I can't wait to help you thrive!

❑ ❑ ❑

HealthType™ and related terminology are concepts of the Shae Group ecosystem (including Shae®, ph360™ and Precision Health Alliance). Used with acknowledgment. This e-book is a personal, general-information resource and is not an official Shae Group publication, certification, or training material. For official information, visit HealthType.org and Shae.ai.